RIDING WILD
HORSES HOME

A Conservative Christian
Apology

Katherine Wade Unthank

MOONDRAWN BOOKS
Lafayette, Indiana

RIDING WILD HORSES HOME

Cover Art: Mary Scott Wallace

ISBN 0-9667594-8-6

Publisher's cataloging-in-Publication
Unthank, Katherine Wade
    Riding wild horses home: a conservative christian apology / Katherine Wade Unthank. - - 1st ed.
    p. cm.
    ISBN 0-9667594-8-6
    1. Christian ethics. 2. Lesbians 3. Unthank, Katherine W. —Biography
241   1999   LCCN 98-88123

THANKS

To Lou Dean Jacobs for her encouragement
and laughter.

To Jeff Sparks for
The New Harmony Project.

To Jane Blaffer Owen for her Poet House.

And especially:
To my mother,
Frances Lynn Underwood Unthank,
for birthing this book;
and for teaching me, in the soulful cadence
of her Southern point of view,
to care deeply about the integrity of my life.

For P,

who fell with me through

frozen darkness

to her own hurt;

and

For Scottie,

who scooped me up

off the bottom line.

"As long as we are on Earth the love that unites us will bring us suffering by our very contact with one another because this love is the resetting of a body of broken bones. Even saints cannot live with saints on this Earth without some anguish; without some pain at the differences that come between them.

There are two things men can do about the pain of disunion. They can love or they can hate. Hatred recoils from the sacrifice and sorrow that are the price of resetting the bones. It refuses the pain of reunion."

Thomas Merton,
New Seeds Of Contemplation

RIDING WILD HORSES HOME

INTRODUCTION

This story is about a pilgrimage I made in January of 1995 after remembering an old promise. Keeping that promise forced me to leave safe sanctuary in the solitude of my wilderness home and go apologize for spiritual violence. Going meant choosing love over hate and that choice paid the price of resetting the bones. It's a story about transcending spiritual woundedness. The actual trip, including air travel, took about eight hours. The transcendence, from the moment of violence to conviction that I needed to go apologize, took about fifteen years.

In my story I use the term, **spiritual rape**. Rape is a violent misuse of power. Spiritual rape is a violent misuse of church power. Spiritual rape happens when the collective power of any church institution is used to condemn an individual in a trust relationship with that institution.

The distinction I make is this: When a church chooses hate the result is spiritual rape. When an individual chooses hate, the result is spiritual violence. Clinically speaking, the level of trauma following a spiritual rape is more severe and, like physical rape, produces the classic symptoms of Chronic Trauma Syndrome. In either case the choice of hate breaks spiritual bones.

I perpetrated spiritual violence and then became a victim of spiritual rape. I'm now a Licensed Professional Counselor in the field of mental health which makes me, in Henri J.M. Nouwen's definition, a wounded healer.

"For the minister is called to recognize the suffering of his time in his own heart and make that recognition the starting point of his service. Whether he tries to enter a dislocated world, relate to a convulsive generation, or speak to a dying man, his service will not be perceived as authentic unless it comes from a heart wounded by the suffering about which he speaks." *The Wounded Healer.*

Resetting broken spiritual bones

requires first of all finding and then going back to mark the unmarked graves where those broken bones wait to be remembered. I gleaned the phrase "unmarked graves" from Jesus, among his words to the Pharisees recorded by Luke.(11:39-44)

"Now you Pharisees clean the outside of the cup and of the dish, but inside you are full of greed and wickedness. You fools! Did not the one who made the outside make the inside also? So give for alms those things that are within; and see, everything will be made clean for you. . . . Woe to you! For you are like unmarked graves, and people walk over them without realizing it."

Marking unmarked graves is a frightening process which begins when an individual consciously chooses to make the difficult journey into personal darkness to remember and name, "those things that are within." These remembrances are the alms God desires. The choice God gives us is to keep our inner darkness and be an unmarked grave or to remember and be made clean. Not an easy choice. Remembering darkness hurts.

In the frightening process of remembering my frozen personal darkness, I thawed in the warmth of God's unconditional love and forgiveness and discovered everything had changed except Jesus. Graceful Jesus, "the same yesterday, today and forever." By His grace I am *not* the same today as I was yesterday or will be tomorrow forever. I've come to understand that profound change is the marker whereby we know divine grace has visited a human soul.

"If we accept this Infant as our God, then we accept our own obligation to grow with Him in a world of arrogant power and travel with Him as He ascends to Jerusalem and to the Cross, which is the denial of power."

Thomas Merton
The Good News Of The Nativity

RIDING WILD HORSES HOME

REMEMBERING ARROGANCE

Travelling through the wilderness of Northwest Colorado to keep an old promise I've long forgotten and recently remembered all I know anymore is this: It's brutally cold outside. My nose hurts because it won't stop running. I can't write about rage until I take responsibility for the rage I've caused. Maybe caused. I don't know how Peggy feels. I've trespassed against her with enough knowing. I need to be careful I don't trespass against her now with an arrogant assumption that I know how she feels. I don't know.

I'm a true descendant of Eve. I have a genuine problem with know-ing. I believe one tiny seed from the fruit she picked and ate off the tree of the knowledge of good and evil passed through the genetic bowels of humankind undigested until birthed into me and then blos-somed into the full arrogant glory of my *KNOWING*.

"You can't be gay and a Christian."

I keep hearing this refrain of my all-knowing youth. I pound the steering wheel screaming anguish out loud in my car. I want to punch my runny nose. As if additional violence will change the past or make any difference. The great patriarchal myth. More power will take care of anything. More money, more sex, more wins, more votes, more house, more view, more prestige, more food, more chocolate, more anything. More power.

Well, maybe more chocolate will help. M&M's and Sudafed. Food for soul and sinuses. What's the matter with me? I felt fine yesterday. Now I'm on the road back to Peggy falling into chocolate addiction and getting sick.

I glance in the rear view mirror at my dog, Agatha, sound asleep on the package shelf. She gives no response to screams of soul anguish. Soul stuff doesn't phase her. Marion Woodman says,

"Dogs . . . mythically, are the guardians between life and death.

They are an intuitive bridge between conscious and unconscious, connectors to the psychoid level of the psyche. Dogs are invaluable to those who love them because their love is total and they mirror their master's inner world, a world with which the master may have lost touch. Experiencing the dog's responses the human being makes the inner connection. They are like us, but other, a step toward the humanization of wild instincts." *The Ravaged Bridegroom*

This mirrors my inner world? What do I see in the mirror? A dog either totally relaxed and trusting the driving source or completely unconscious to the danger. I don't know which mirrors my inner world. I open the bag of M&M's. The sound of crinkle wrap brings the sleeping Agatha to full attention, off the shelf, her cold nose immediately on my arm.

"What?," I ask.

She speaks her human vowel. "Oooooooooooo."

She prefers the red ones.

I love my dog and she loves me, thereby mirroring my inner world. This is why I believe M&M's are soul food. I give her the red ones. It feels like a practical thing to do on the way to keeping a difficult promise.

RIDING WILD HORSES HOME

"This is a spiritual fact. It is that those whom we have wronged will always represent God to us. When we meet them, it is as though we were meeting God. Thank God if, when this is so, our hearts are truly humbled before him."

> Watchman Nee
> **A Table In The Wilderness**

RIDING WILD HORSES HOME

REMEMBERING VIOLENCE

Agatha and I began our journey at night in winter under a new moon. New moon in the wilderness gives Earth her purest darkness. Driving through that darkness requires an alert vigilance to avoid hitting wildlife on the road. Wildlife moves around at night, especially in the hours just before dawn.

I remember my first drive through this isolation near the Colorado/Utah border, desperately searching for a safe place to hide. God carried my frozen, wounded soul out here. Years later I finally heard her screaming, but that meant progress. I could hear the voices naming my rage. As we're driving away I credit the wilderness and the Goddess I met in this wilderness for the remembrance of these voices. I'm also clutching the memory of my violence against Peggy, holding that pain in my heart to keep my purpose for this journey clear. I had to remember my violence before I could remember the promise.

I had tried to write about spiritual rape in a detached, clinically professional sort of way, aloof being my lifeline of action since that wound robbed me of interpersonal trust. In the acute phase of Rape Trauma Syndrome

I met criteria for a Controlled Impact Reaction. Any rape victim knows the internal craziness which follows that violence and the compelling need to regain some sense of control at all costs. In my post rape craziness, that's when Aloof was born. Aloof in me wrestles with God. Aloof looks powerful but actually, I've learned, he feels terrified and doesn't want to be Aloof anymore. He wants to change. I want to let him change but we're both stuck.

An established authoress read my first, aloof, draft of this book and suggested I bring my own story up front. That's when I learned Aloof feels terrified, but we danced together in the bright light of telling our story. Aloof let me hold him and he calmed in my softness. That's when he whispered, "I don't want to be Aloof anymore." So we danced and wrote a second draft attached to rage.

Then the established authoress said, "You've got to get rid of the anger in this. People won't read it."

Aloof stormed off to be aloof and seized control again. I've been trying for years since to get him to dance but, he says, he knows what he knows.

In the vast wilderness where I live wild horses still roam. I've seen them twice in seven years. Magnificent animals. One day, I read that people are adopting wild horses from the government with promises to feed and care for them and, instead, sell our wild horses to the European market for horse meat. This enraged me.

"If that's not rape nothing is," I said out loud. Alone in my house nobody heard me but Aloof and when he tried to stay aloof my soul shouted at him, "Get A Life!"

We were both stunned by her fury but pleased to hear her voice. Aloof cringed but couldn't take his eyes off her. She didn't say any more that day, but she paced back and forth in what is normally Aloof's space. He didn't let her take over his space. He had no choice in the matter. She simply was there. Raw, energized power. Pacing. Aloof liked her. After all, we both knew he really did want to get a life.

We're at this impasse. Soul pacing her rage in silence and Aloof cringing in fascinated terror. He looks at me, knowing what he knows, with wide eyes that implore me to do something. I approach her in her agitation. She stops and looks at me with narrowed eyes.

"Good," she says sarcastically, "You showed up."

I don't know what to say, but, as she stands there and doesn't resume pacing, I stand too.

"What do you know?" she demands.

I glance at Aloof, still cringing in his fascination. She turns my face with one hand to look at her face.

"He knows what he knows.

What do you know?"

Soul's touch electrifies me, bolting from the base of my spine to the tips of my hair. Her eyes look like rainbows spiraling into forever. I fall into the rainbows forever. I think, "I know what you know."

"Exactly," she whispers, pleased. I realize she has her mouth by my ear. She says, "Be here now."

I pace in Soul's space knowing what she knows. Aloof wants to climb down and join me. I tell him to stay where he is. He doesn't like this response. I say, "If you're Aloof then be aloof."

He starts down again. I repeat, firmly, "I am here now. If you're unhappy about that, then, you aren't aloof anymore are you?"

He looks at me, startled, and then he disappears.

I pace in Soul's space knowing what she knows, remembering what she knows. I close my eyes and see the rainbows forever. I remember Peggy. She rises to me through soul's rainbows more than memory. She rises with the energy of deeply rooted love, grinning, riding a stampede of red rage that softens to the singular, southern heart touched blue of her eyes.

I realize I've lost Peggy. I cut her off in the frozen wake of spiritual rape when Aloof took control and shut everything down. I hate that, feeling rage flare her red nostrils and stomp her powerful hooves. I expect Aloof to reappear but in his place come tears. It's like sitting in an ice well with warm tears filling the frozen space. I cry into hands covering my face. Then I hear the memory of my own voice echoing in the frozen well.

"You can't be gay and a Christian."

Alarmed, I drop my hands and look at this memory. My young, arrogant face fifteen years ago looks back at me.

"You can't be gay and a Christian," she repeats.

I stare at her. She raises her eyebrows at me, undaunted.

"I thought you ought to know," she says. "I have the key."

"The key to what?"

She laughs. "To everything, of course."

"May I have this key?"

"I just gave it to you," she tells me impatiently.

I suddenly feel old and profoundly tired and start to turn away.

"You can't be gay and a Christian," she repeats slowly, making sure I see the determination in her eyes. And then she disappears. Her words, my voice echo in the frozen well.

"You can't be gay and a Christian."

"You can't be gay and a Christian."

"You can't be gay and a Christian."

I said that to Peggy and she believed me.

I said that to her? The memory of that violence stampedes my rage into horror trampling through all aloof control rushing at me a relentless, crushing weight.

"Oh, my God, Peggy believed me."

Soul puts her mouth next to my ear. "And this is love?"

RIDING WILD HORSES HOME

"Knowing God's heart means consistently, radically and very concretely to announce and reveal that God is love and only love and that every time fear, isolation, or despair begin to invade the human soul this is not something that comes from God."

Henri J.M. Nouwen
In The Name Of Jesus

RIDING WILD HORSES HOME

REMEMBERING A PROMISE

Driving out of this Northwest Colorado wilderness on my way back to Peggy I read conservative Christian bumper stickers that say stuff like, "I know the future and God wins." I cringe. Meeting reminders of my old conservative Christian arrogance through the medium of dust covered bumper stickers I feel like an old pile of conservative Christian road kill. "God wins" doesn't bother me. It's the, "I know the future" part that pierces to my marrow echoing, "I know you can't be gay and a Christian, you can't be gay and a Christian, you can't be gay and a Christian." And this is love? Bumper sticker conviction. I want a bumper sticker that says, "All I know is that God is God and I'm not."

God does win. God says God is love and that love never fails. So, love wins. When rage trampled over me, crushed by conviction face down in the parched earth of my wilderness, I remembered that about God. I remembered Peggy's soul woven through my soul in love.

I also remembered we argued a lot, the energy between us so electric we had to do something with it. She was, sexually, gay in the closet of closets and spiritually searching. I was, sexually, repressed in the arrogant celibacy of conservative Christianity and spiritually on the threshold of rape. So we shared our powerful love for each other in powerful verbal intercourse which looked and sounded like arguing.

But we never argued at the quarries. That was my favorite place to be with her. We hiked together through the woods back to abandoned stone quarries where everyone swam and sunbathed naked. We baked our bodies and slept on slabs of limestone surrounding beautiful water so deep nobody knew what lay at bottom.

Turned out to be toxic waste. PCB's. One of the largest EPA Superfund cleanup sites in the nation created by Westinghouse dumping old transformers into the abandoned quarries for twenty years. I suppose, in the 50's, it must have seemed like a good idea. Upon discovery in the 80's nobody at Westinghouse had much publicly to say. I wrote for the statewide newspaper by that time so I can tell you firsthand about the profound silence of Westinghouse. As one among generations of young people who unconsciously swam and sunbathed naked in the toxic waste of Westinghouse I can also tell you we shared the denial offered by that profound silence. To my knowledge, no swimmer or sunbather ever came forward to sue Westinghouse for damages.

First, I guess, because getting to the quarries meant trespassing on private property. POSTED NO TRESPASSING. I remember the sign. Fading words face up on the ground next to a wire fence long since stomped down by 60's and 70's and early 80's swimmers and sunbathers. NO TRESPASSING. A landmark indicating our destination in the deep woods was near.

Second, the news that you've been swimming around in toxic waste feels unnerving. We entered an idyllic world out there in our youth. The place held us like a cathedral in muted silence of hushed conversations, echoed splashing, fragrant, humid warmth, every human body and soul bare and open to the blue sky. God and Earth loved us there. She embraced our free-spirited presence. I see the experience now as the moment when grace entered my arrogant knowing to prepare me for the journey through frozen darkness into this wilderness where I first heard her voice. I felt the divine in that place, but did not know her name. Recently, she has begun whispering to me.

God and Earth loved us there. We loved in return and returned again and again. Generation after generation drawn to the sacred like a rite of passage, an unwritten ritual of vital youth contained in that cathedral place. Discovering the desecration of toxic waste; hearing the news that our pure Earth space had been victimized by toxic rape long before we knew her was a shattering reality. Somebody had dumped the threat of cancer into our trusting innocence.

Nobody wanted to talk about it. I didn't. Profound silence shared by victim and rapist. Somebody at Westinghouse probably just thought it was a good idea. That's all. No harm intended to generation after generation. Those whose naked bodies were prone to soaking up PCB induced cancer will have to remember that. No harm intended. An administrative mistake. Those who escape cancer can feel lucky. We were all robbed of the true divine and our innocence. But grace met me in that unconsciously violent and beautiful place. She began preparing me for church violence; even though at that time, I still believed God and the church were the same thing.

Peggy is the one who first took me to the quarries. I never went with anyone else. The two of us never went alone. Peggy travels in team. Often, however, we would be alone together on a limestone slab while her entourage swam or sunbathed elsewhere. Peggy and I couldn't argue there. We swam and sunbathed and bonded in that warm, forbidden place.

One day I asked her about her first female lover, how that had come about. She told me the story. Then she said,

"It was a mistake."

She was sunbathing a little above me on a higher rock, her eyes closed. I had asked my question while sunbathing with my eyes closed.

"They have all been mistakes," she added.

I sat up, startled, and looked at her face, her closed eyes now level with mine.

"All?" I said. But that wasn't what I wanted to say. She turned her head and opened her laughing eyes.

"Not so many." Her face inches away. Her eyes so southern blue.

I said,

"I don't ever want to be a mistake in your life."

"You won't be," she replied, gently.

We both meant it in that sacred, innocent place.

But we were both wrong. We didn't know the toxic waste that lay at bottom.

I remember after saying, "You can't be gay and a Christian," she drove me home in silence and dropped me off in silence. No anger. She would have voiced anger. That's why we argue well. We both voice anger as easily as breathing. Just silence. I got out of her car, carried the silence inside the house and sat with it. Later, she called to break the silence. She called to tell me to go outside and see the rainbow.

Fifteen years later, in wilderness solitude, I lifted my face from the parched earth and wrote,

Standing beneath a rainbow
miles apart
except our hearts
and you knowing what I could
not;
you called to be sure
I saw the promise,
that I shared the divine sky
and, choosing God's own colors,
softly thereby
you kissed me as deeply
as any lover could.
And though we now stand
as we once stood
miles apart;

all my soul's rainbows whisper
recalling my heart
to remember what you knew
that I could not.

In early autumn, after the rainbow, I had said to Peggy, "I wish I
could tell you it's O.K. with God
for you to be gay, but I know it's
not. If God ever shows me I'm
wrong about that, I promise I'll tell
you."

I promise I'll tell you.
I promise I'll tell you.
God won.

God threw me a rainbow I
would find fifteen years later
attached to a lifeline still floating
on the surface of my unconscious
sea of arrogance. A lifeline plung-

ing down, down, down, down to terrifying depths. The moment I became conscious of my spiritual violence against Peggy I had to grab that lifeline or lose it forever and wander lost on soul ground that instantly transformed from seawater to dry desert. Which is where I, in fact, live.

This particular wilderness in Northwest Colorado used to be the bottom of Earth's oceans. The dinosaurs died here. Their remains lie beneath the earth in oil and coal. Fossil fuel. Fossil fuel has to be dug out, pumped out, forced out violently or that latent energy won't move at all. Fossil fuel waits, passively, for discovery. Humans fight wars over it. The souls of the dinosaurs must have some last, great pre-historic laugh over that. Pre-historic. As if nothing counts historically before humans arrived. God wiped humankind out once before on account of such arrogance. Noah built the ark and saved our remnant. Maybe dinosaurs were too big to make the boat and because of their size and our arrogance they died along with that first batch of us when we pissed God off. That time before the first rainbow. Maybe dinosaurs never got to see rainbows. Who knows? I don't.

All I know is that Peggy made sure I saw a rainbow and I gave her a promise and they both waited, passively, beneath the surface at the end of that lifeline for discovery fifteen years later. My fossil fuel. Energy for the journey. A lifeline pulling in focused direction to a specific action. A simple task. A promise to be kept. Grab it and hold on or let go and wander aimlessly in the desert, forever on the dry surface until death by thirst.

On the road to keep this old promise I offer a toast to the anguished souls of dinosaurs. Anguish, I know, because of my anguish. The drink is anguish or nothing. Fossil fuel. Energy out of pre-historic loss, pain and death. Buried anguish. Brought to the surface by historic loss, pain and death. Marking unmarked graves. Amazing grace.

Again, I feel Soul's mouth next to my ear, whispering, but her voice is His voice asking, "Will you drink this cup? Will you remember me?" And I think,

"This is love."

*"Does anyone have the foggiest idea
what sort of power we so blithely
invoke? . . . The churches are children
playing on the floor with their chemistry
sets, mixing up a batch of TNT to kill a
Sunday morning. It is madness to wear
ladies straw hats and velvet hats to
church; we should all be wearing crash
helmets. Ushers should issue life
preservers and signal flares; they
should lash us to our pews. For the
sleeping God may wake someday and
take offense, or the waking god may
draw us out to where we can never
return."*

Annie Dillard
Teaching A Stone To Talk

RIDING WILD HORSES HOME

REMEMBERING ANGELA

Agatha is sleeping off her allotment of red M&M's and I am hearing Peggy's voice as I drive, the way she sounded when I called to ask if I could come. I don't know how Peggy feels but I know her dog just died. She told me about it over the phone. A "no brainer" decision, she said, to have a suffering animal put down. I wanted to say, "Yes, but, what about your heart?" What about her heart? As if I have a right to ask. I didn't ask.

Of course I could come. Peggy's gracious, southern voice welcomes me as if we'd only been apart a week rather than a decade. Everything that could have happened to my all knowing youth has happened in that time resulting in this specific journey out of my frozen wilderness into the unknown. Her willingness to receive me now feels like being wrapped in an old, familiar coat which I appreciate here in middle age, vulnerable without my youthful armor of arrogant knowing.

I have never taken Peggy's willingness to receive me for granted; the miracle of her coming around the corner of the house that summer searching for me; looking up from my vegetable garden and there she was. Unexpected. Unannounced. She was then, as she is now, the queen of her world.

Beautiful. Athletic. Intelligent. Wealthy. Generous above all else. Terrified of dying.

And she sought me that summer day wanting to talk about God. I suppose we both thought I had the answers.

"You can't be gay and a Christian."

That's the good news I gave a lost goddess in search of a way home.

Still, fifteen years later, she receives me. Her dog is dead. She tries, on the phone, to be cavalier in tone as if, "it's just a dog" can be implied if not said in truth. Peggy doesn't speak untruth. Hiding truth in silence is her way of lying. So she changes the subject and asks about Angela.

"I don't hear from Angela

anymore."

"What happened?"

Exactly like Peggy, immediately getting to the point before I even know a point needs to be gotten to. She calls this the bottom line. She must have asked me a hundred times during our arguments that quarry summer, "So, what's the bottom line?"

I look down at my dog soul reflection and ask her, "So, Agatha, what exactly is the bottom line?" Agatha, wisely, keeps her silence. At this precise moment the bottom line is that when I arrive, when I see Peggy again I'll have to answer her question, "What happened?"

For years I had no name for what happened.

I heard about Angela and Ric

before I met them. I knew Ric had been diagnosed with cancer. A Melanoma. When I arrived in the mountain community where they lived I learned that everyone expected him to be healed. People believed this miracle would happen because the elders of the church Ric pastored announced to the congregation that God had told them Ric would, in fact, be healed. They anointed him with oil, laid hands on him and prayed. From that moment, I was told, everyone believed through faith that the healing had been accomplished.

When I met Ric he was still active, going to work. Two weeks later he could barely get out of bed and come downstairs. The spiritual environment in Ric and

Angela's home fascinated me. I felt drawn to them and wanted to be there. Day and night people came and went constantly, especially those elders, praying with Ric, praying with Angela for Ric, always praising God for his healing. I observed and listened. I remember the day at Angela's house when she broke down and told my sister and me she couldn't hide her feelings anymore. Her husband was obviously dying leaving her with three small kids to take care of and she was scared.

Ric died.

He was 29-years-old. I went to his funeral. I heard people there say they expected him to rise from death during the service because, how could the elders have been wrong?

Ric didn't rise.

Six months later I was with Angela in her living room when one of those elders, also one of Angela's closest friends, was sent to inform her the church leadership had decided the reason Ric died was because her faith in his healing had faltered. She simply hadn't had enough faith to allow God to work a miracle for her husband.

Sitting there, silently, I felt stunned by his words to her and enraged. I felt what I witnessed there that day very deeply, but I had no name for it.

As years passed I watched Angela turn her back on the church and God and walk away. What choice was she given? To stay and accept responsibility for her husband's death? Could she be expected to trust a spiritual community which, in her hour of greatest need, turned on her with such an accusation? Could she even trust her own faith in solitude?

One day, before Ric died, I went to their house so Angela could cut my hair. Grace provided a rare moment for me because nobody else was there that morning. While she cut my hair I talked, whined actually, about my life condition as a recent college graduate with no clear future and no job prospects beyond cooking in the local Mexican food restaurant. Ric made his way downstairs, obviously in great pain. He sat at the end of the couch in the living room with his elbows on his knees and his head in his hands. I was aware of his presence but thought him to be lost in his own world. When I walked past him to the front door, however, he said, "It sounds like you're having a rough time." He lifted his head, looked at me and added, "There are bigger waves down the road."

What could I say? There's nothing like the perspective of a 29-year-old dying man to put living in right context. Whenever the waves swell above my head I remember his eyes and his words and I sail on. "There are bigger waves down the road." I still believe that's so. But the wave of church violence that was to crush my soul left me falling through a frozen darkness, paralyzed.

I learned the name of what the church did to Angela much later, after the church did similar violence to me. Horribly damaged and doing greater damage to others in pitiful attempts to gain control of my life I floundered in the wake of that violence many years before seeking professional help. My therapist asked, "What's the darkest, blackest memory you carry in your heart?" She listened to my story and said, "You've been spiritually raped."

At last, I could call what happened by name and mark the grave.

"In the long, long process of healing our wounds by discovering their spiritual meaning, we discover who we are."

Marion Woodman
Leaving My Father's House

RIDING WILD HORSES HOME

REMEMBERING RAGE

What do I say? How much do I say about spiritual rape to a person I've spiritually abused? I owe Peggy an apology and a promise kept, not a sip from my cup of anguish.

"It's a long story. I don't want to talk about it on the phone."

"Is that what you're coming to tell me about?"

"I'm coming to keep a promise. Do you remember the promise I made to you?"

She doesn't remember the promise. Her dog has just died. A dog I never knew. We're trying to connect with loose threads left hanging and frayed over a fifteen year gap. Peggy probably could not possibly care less about an ancient promise. But I don't know how Peggy feels. I can't keep thinking I do. I say,

"I'm sorry about your dog."

Her cavalier voice in reply about going to pick out a new puppy soon sounds small and fragile. I want to enter her grief with a gift of hope, with the good news of an all loving God I failed to give before. I want to tell her what I said to my friend, Jeff, when his daughter's rabbit died.

Jeff shared with me how hard it was telling his grieving child her dead rabbit wasn't going to heaven.

And I asked him,

"How do you know that?"

"Because animals don't go to heaven. They aren't saved."

"How did your daughter take this news?"

"She got angry and didn't believe me."

I think I heard a dinosaur chuckle.

"Good for her. I don't believe you either."

"You believe animals are saved?" He asked, rather hopefully as I recall.

"I believe animals don't need to be saved. They've never trespassed against God. Trespassing against God is a uniquely human endeavor."

Jeff's face lightens up which, I think, makes Jeff a neat guy. He likes getting torqued theologically. I give his theology deep rolfing. Still, he's church bound and stumbles around hamstrung with "the principles of men". He says, sadly,

"I just wish I could show her something in the Bible about that."

"Show her Psalm 36:6."

But I didn't tell Peggy this story. How do you say to somebody you've told, "you can't be gay and a Christian", that dead dogs go to heaven?

What happened doesn't matter, I tell myself driving along the highway cramming M&Ms in my face. Now matters. Telling Peggy I trespassed against God when I said, "You can't be gay and a Christian", and she believed me and turned away from Jesus and his open, loving arms. Keeping a promise to say I was wrong about that is what matters.

I imagine trying to make this point to Peggy and laugh out loud. As if she'll stop asking questions when I say it. As if she'll stop anywhere short of the bottom line. Which, I realize, is why I'm suddenly getting more ill with every passing mile. To face her again I have to face everything that happened all the way down to the bottom line. That's a lot. That's what Aloof keeps me from having to do. That's why I break out in hives and have to take Cortisone.

It's as if from the moment I said to her, "If God ever shows me I'm wrong about that . . . ," God began putting me through what it would take for me to know I was wrong. For a soul as arrogant as mine, it took nothing short of spiritual rape. For me to be able to choose to keep my promise required a journey through that frozen darkness.

That's a hard thought to take. That idea sucks the red right out of my rage. I'm on the way to keep a promise that going through the hell of spiritual rape empowered me to keep. I'm on the way to apologize for violence that going through the violence of spiritual rape allowed me to recognize. If not for spiritual rape, maybe I'd still be lost in the arrogance of unconscious knowing.

Whoa. Hard revelation here on the road. Hard to stay with. Even M&Ms don't help. I blow my nose. Again. Agatha twitches in her sleep next to me. Dreaming. I remember a dream I had before my spiritual rape. In the dream a voice said to me, "You're not poetic, you're noetic." When I woke, I looked up the word "noetic". I'd never heard it before.

"Of or existing or originating in the intellect. Interested in intellectual activity. An intellectual person."

Weird, learning words in dreams. That happened before I

knew anything about Carl Jung or Marion Woodman or Helen Luke.

Remembering that dream I remembered what my friend Tara had said to me the last time we saw each other, a few months before my spiritual rape. She said, "You always have been too intelligent for your own damn good." Fifteen years ago, I took that as a compliment. Fifteen years ago I couldn't hear these warnings of danger.

"Let those who have ears to hear, hear," Jesus often says. And I thought I was hearing every word. No, I KNEW I was hearing every word. Noetic.

Knowing. That's even the name of the perfume I wear. Jeez. This is just too sick, I think, driving ever closer to facing Peggy with my apology for *knowing*.

Too sick and I'm sick and wondering if this journey to promise keeping is necessary after all. I felt fine in my familiar wilderness. This liminal space, this birth canal I'm moving through getting to Peggy again is making me sick. Just beam me into Peggy's living room, please. Forgo all this journey getting from one place to another. It's not the promise that's hard, it's what comes to light crossing the threshold to keep it that rises through the tissues of my body and demands attention. Running out my nose. I hear soul chuckling. "Running out my knows." Her very divine sense of humor accompanies these revelations.

Sense of humor left me in the frozen darkness after spiritual rape. Rape always produces powerlessness and powerlessness always produces rage. Rage has no sense of humor. Rage is into having power. Rage is into having control. Rage replaces a victim's powerless reality with an illusion of control. That's what Aloof knows. "If I can control rage, I can control anything," he says and did for years.

They companioned me faithfully, Rage and Aloof; one silent the other always on the surface and in control. Rage motivated everything I did, good or bad. Aloof smoothed the surface and held the energy there so that nothing ever got through to me, good or bad. I earned a Masters degree motivated by rage. After 12 years of celibacy I became sexually active motivated by rage. I wrote the first three drafts of this book motivated by rage. Great energy in Rage. She never lets me down. Aloof keeps her contained, but, I can't remain Aloof and keep my promise to Peggy. Getting back to Peggy and the bottom line means facing Rage. Aloof keeps me safe from her, knowing what he knows. All these years I've known about Rage, what she is, how she grows more powerful every hour she's kept in darkness behind Aloof.

I explain Rage to my clients. She

is all unfelt feelings never given life, unattended, unheard, and shoved back into a hard inner core of darkness. She stomps at the parched wilderness there, seething with power. People visualize Rage in endless ways. In me she's the wild horses. The herd multiplying year after year. When Aloof disappeared and Rage trampled over me with the revelation of my trespass against God, my violence to Peggy I thought, face down in the parched wilderness, that perhaps Rage had all escaped. Now, on this road to Peggy, face up and having seized the lifeline, I can see Rage in the shadows waiting to be ridden and named one by one before they'll serve me in the light.

No wonder I'm sick and counting the cost of this promise keeping journey. I long for the return of Aloof and what he knows which is that if I turn around now and forget this trip he'll return to contain Rage and preserve my familiar wilderness. Choice. Because God trespasses against no one, I must choose.

I'm out of M&Ms. I stop the car and let Agatha out to do dog hygiene. She performs these chores quickly because it's cold and Agatha always chooses not to be cold. I envy her simple choices. I envy her unbroken communion with God. No human hassles. No trespass issues against the Divine. Certainly she's been trespassed against.

Watching her I wonder how she deals with that past violence. Agatha is a death row dog. When they called me about her she was due to be put down in an hour. The shelter personnel were desperate to find her a home because she is such an endearing little soul. Her first owners had let her get pregnant in her first heat and then drowned her puppies in the river. Our animal control officer found her lying on the highway bridge over the river where her puppies died nearly dead herself with mastitis.

How can she be so gentle? Where is her rage? What allows her, after suffering the violence of human arrogance, to trust and bond with me, an arrogant human? She's a mystery, like the Trinity, beyond what I can know. The mystery wags her tail. I let her back into the warm car and go in search of M&Ms.

Rage stampedes after me. Choice. Love or hate? The pain of reunion or not? Turn back or go on? I really am sick. Peggy will understand that. I can promise to come another time. Another promise to keep a promise she doesn't even remember me making the first time fifteen years ago. That sounds exceptionally rational. I hear an echo of her young, southern voice, "So, Kitty, what's the bottom line?"

Do I leave her with, "You can't be gay and a Christian"? Did God allow me to be crushed by spiritual rape so I'd be able to keep this promise to Peggy? Did I experience all that just to have this moment of choice? Is standing here making choices in a funky gas station restroom my life's equivalent of Jesus choosing the cross in the garden of Gethsemani? It would be.

"In our moments of choice how do we know that we are obeying the voice of truth? We can only do our best to discriminate our motives, free ourselves from conventional opinions, watch our dreams, use our intelligence, together with our intuition, weigh the values involved and the effects on other people, and then act wholeheartedly from the deepest level we know.

If our choice proves to be a mistake, it will be a creative mistake - a mistake leading to consciousness."

Helen M. Luke
Kaleidoscope

RIDING WILD HORSES HOME

REMEMBERING KIMBERLY

Fortunately, the Goddess inspired somebody to create two pounder bags of M&M's for 20th century people who experience Gethsemani moments in gas stations. I understand why Peter, James and John fell asleep on Jesus three times in that garden. Choosing consciousness when faced with the pain of an impending crucifixion is tough. Falling asleep is a great sedative for Gethsemani level psychic agony. So is eating two pounds of sugar in the form of M&M's, an option Peter,

James and John did not have.

I get back into the car with Agatha and start the engine to keep us both warm. Like a good little soul mirror dog, she's buried herself under her blanket. I'd like to crawl under there with her and fall asleep on this promise keeping journey to Peggy and the bottom line. I know if I do, Peggy will just ask me, again, "What happened?"

Shit happened. Now, there's a bumper sticker worth its glue. Lately I've seen the conservative Christian counter punch bumper sticker that says, "Blessings Happen." I guess the conservative Christian crowd is too busy being offended by the word "shit" to realize that blessings quite often come in the guise of shit happening and that God shovels it.

Trees have always been a powerful life source for me. I used to walk around alone in the woods singing songs to them in my childhood. I pay attention to trees. Before my spiritual rape my life had grown to be like the tree in the Bible that stopped bearing fruit. When ordered to tear the tree down and take it out of the garden, the gardener said, "No, let me dig a trench around it and fill the trench with manure (read shit) and then, after a year, if it doesn't bear fruit I'll tear it down." Shit happens to get at the root of things. Some of us require deeper shit than others. Spiritual rape is deep shit, but when someone claiming to be a Christian starts bearing rotten fruit like, "You can't be gay and a Christian," deep shit needs to happen. Fortunately, in the trenches of spiritual rape, shit got through to me and I changed. I came to my senses in the wilderness, but I'm still in the garden (read gas station). Blessings in deep shit happen.

Answering "what happened?" matters, then, since I had to go through it all to be able to make this choice to keep a promise to Peggy or not. I have to shovel back through all the shit to get to the bottom line which seems to wait for me where she waits for me.

What happened began the week Peggy left in early fall after the summer she came to me around the corner of the house. She left knowing what I could not and in that prescience she wrote me, "I worry. I wonder where your life and the Lord will lead you."

She left with my promise before God and our rainbow and so the Goddess began, laying shovel to the roots of my spiritual arrogance.

Kimberly came into our lives in early fall after the summer Peggy came around the corner of the house. She joined our home Bible study when she was eight months pregnant. Soon after her first visit she began dropping by the house often and explained her story to Angela and me.

She was single, trying to decide

whether or not to keep the baby after it was born. She'd arranged for her child to be adopted through a Christian adoption agency in another state, so, she soon left us for that place to await delivery. Her options remained open. We didn't know if she'd return with or without a baby.

The phone call came late at night. A boy. She didn't want to give him up. She had 72 hours to decide. An indescribably brutal, agonizing time. Hours spent on the phone. Tears upon tears. She came home alone.

As we shared her grieving process I learned more about the journey which led to that terrible moment of decision. The father of her son was a married leader of a church she'd attended in another town. She respected his counsel. Both he and his wife befriended her. He began coming to her apartment alone. A three-year affair developed which resulted in her pregnancy. Kimberly left town in order to protect him. No one in that church ever knew of this man's involvement with Kimberly. His wife gave birth to a daughter soon after Kimberly gave birth to a son.

Kimberly left his church, returned to her parent's community and joined our church with a full confession of her circumstances. We lived in a large community. She could have hidden herself away there or anywhere else she chose. Instead, Kimberly owned her mistake and stayed in Christian fellowship while facing the consequences.

Although the father of her child obviously misused his position of spiritual leadership in pursuing a sexual relationship with Kimberly and she suffered devastating consequences because of their misconduct, she didn't become a spiritual rape victim until she entered our church community.

Two things happened within six months after the birth and adoption of Kimberly's son. As in every spiritual rape, I have no idea and neither does she what went on behind the scenes which led to the first blow.

A week before Christmas Kimberly's roommate suddenly announced she had to move out, "Because," she said, "people in the church had advised her that living with Kimberly was not a healthy situation." This woman had known Kimberly from childhood. She attended our Bible study and brought Kimberly there the first time. She had traveled with Kimberly out of state to wait for the birth of this child. She companioned Kimberly through it all. They'd signed a year's lease together on the apartment they shared. Suddenly, she pulled out of the relationship because it had been labeled, "unhealthy", by the church.

Kimberly had two weeks to find

another apartment, another roommate or pay the entire rent. Angela
submitted a request for emergency
assistance from the church Deacon's
fund on Kimberly's behalf. They
turned her down.

So I watched Kimberly, like I'd
watched Angela, devastated with
grief being rejected by her spiritual
community in an hour of greatest
need. At this point in Kimberly's
spiritual rape process, however, the
judgement passed against her
wasn't yet as clear as in Angela's
case. She just felt confused and
numb. She used the urgency of
the situation to help her ignore
Christmas. She didn't feel like
doing Christmas that year. She
ignored everything, including the

church, and focused on meeting her immediate need for new housing.

Generous non-church people in our community helped Kimberly re-arrange her life over the holidays. The Bible study helped her move. Our lives went on but an unavoidable, ugly shadow now hung over Kimberly's situation. People were taking sides behind the scenes. Angela stopped going to church altogether. The Bible study broke apart. In the end, the judgement of our church leadership came to light.

One Sunday the pastor preached a sermon out of the Old Testament about Hannah and her son Samuel. The point of his sermon was this: that Hannah made a mistake giving Samuel up to Eli for adoption because even though she had prayed about it and believed she was doing the right thing, it is never the will of God, under any circumstances, for a mother to give her child away.

He drove that message home clearly, repeatedly, pointedly and purposefully. Kimberly walked out of church that day and never returned. She hasn't joined another church community since.

Peggy visited and met Kimberly in the spring, after all this happened. I came home from work and discovered her teaching Kimberly how to play Pac Man, both of them drinking Kahlua and Cream. Having Peggy back felt like a rainbow after our long winter storm of grief and church violence. But Peggy never knew about Kimberly's spiritual rape, or Angela's either. We didn't have a name for it then. I was still the blind, arrogant queen of conservative Christian knowing unaware that my spiritual rape began when Kimberly's spiritual rape happened.

I pat Agatha under her blanket, back the car out and return to the highway. My own story waits to be remembered. I'm eyeball to eyeball with the wild horses, staring me down, snorting their hot rage into the frozen air.

RIDING WILD HORSES HOME

"First, do not run away from your inner feelings even when they seem fearful. By following them through you will understand them better and be more free to look for new ways when the old ways run into a blank wall.

Second, when you explore in depth your unruly and wild emotions you will be confronted with your sinful self. This confrontation should not lead to despair but should set you free to receive the compassion of God without whom no healing is possible."

Henri J.M. Nouwen
Genesee Diary

RIDING WILD HORSES HOME

REMEMBERING MALEDICTUS

I always watch for wild horses, but they're reclusive and seldom seen from the road. In winter though, if snow is deep and constant, they'll sometimes wander down in search of food. They come closer to us reluctantly, I believe. Wild horses seem to find humans unsatisfactory neighbors. Given our propensity for arrogant violence, I think wild horses behave sensibly. So, although I watch, I have little hope of catching sight of them on this winter journey. Within, however, they're clearly on a rampage clamoring for my attention.

I watched spiritual rape happen to Angela and Kimberly, then spiritual rape happened to me. Falling through a ten-year Rape Reaction Response, through the Acute Phase and Chronic Trauma Syndrome absolutely frozen with unresolved rage, I suffered severe relational dysfunction, sexual dysfunction and somatisized anxiety disorder waking up with panic attacks and breaking out in hives so pervasive I required cortisone to reduce the swelling. As these memories rise my agitated depression rises with them. I like to drive when I feel agitated. Something to do staying busy getting somewhere else. I've driven thousands of agitated miles in years of frozen darkness getting nowhere. Now here I am getting sicker by the minute on my way to keep a promise to Peggy who wants to know, "What happened?"

My spiritual rape happened like all spiritual rapes happen, over time behind the scenes in the darkness. Then, suddenly, the collective condemnation of the church came to light and raped me. It feels like a long story but that's because the wound is so old now and familiar. In the long fall through frozen darkness, I became what the church named me. Unhealthy. Remembering this promise to Peggy is my key to freedom from the power of that violent darkness. Keeping this promise to Peggy I choose love over hate.

Before God carried me into the wilderness to meet the Goddess, my friend Jeff invited me to the New Harmony Project, an annual gathering of selected writers, actors and directors focusing on the development of plays and screenplays in New Harmony, Indiana. Jeff gave me a great gift of light in New Harmony. I went there the first time six years after my spiritual rape, six years into the wound, bearing the fruit of the wound, becoming what the church had named me. In all those years frozen in destructive darkness, the only times I felt the warmth of creative light was in New Harmony. New Harmony is a Goddess place, created by Jane Owen in whom the Goddess moves powerfully. She can be seen there, a beautiful woman in a big floppy hat riding around in a golf cart tending the endless gardens all over her town. She hands out flowers and smiles to visiting friends and strangers alike as if we were all just long lost family returned home at last. Which, when we can finally see the Goddess, is what we are.

I breathed the light of New Harmony and felt my frozen soul slowly turn toward the warmth of healing. Two messages found me there. The first from Thomas Merton, a quote on a plaque at the end of a sidewalk outside the Roofless Chapel.

"As long as we are on Earth, the love that unites us will bring us suffering by our very contact with one another because this love is a resetting of a body of broken bones- even saints cannot live with saints on this Earth without some anguish; without some pain at the difference that comes between them.

There are two things men can do about the pain of disunion- they can love or they can hate. Hatred recoils from the sacrifice and sorrow that are the price of resetting the bones - it refuses the pain of reunion."

Reading this my choices between love and hate became clear, but until I entered the wilderness and the Goddess reminded me of my promise to Peggy I couldn't see the point of reunion. I thought, for a long time after first reading this quote, that the disunion was between me and my rapist, the church. I could not reconcile myself to reunion with the violent church. When I heard the Goddess the way to complete the circle in reunion came clear. The resetting of a body of broken bones has nothing to do with violent church institutions, it has to do with disunioned hearts and souls woven together in Goddess love. The seed of Thomas Merton's quote planted in my soul in New

Harmony bore its fruit years later as I wrestled with sacrifice and sorrow on the way to keep my promise to Peggy.

The second message of New Harmony came to me from Walt Wongren who gave a talk one Sunday morning to a small group of us gathered at The Barn to worship. He explained the power of the dictus, the spoken word. I learned that humans, alone in all of God's creation, have the godlike power of dictus, the spoken word. We can speak benedictus, which is a blessing or maledictus which is a curse. Listening to Walt that spring morning I understood that the church had spoken maledictus against me and I had been excommunicated under the power of a curse. Not just any old curse, but a curse spoken by church leaders against me in the name of Jesus Christ. That's a violent misuse of power. That's not just flesh and blood stuff, that's spiritual wickedness in high places. Six years later, sitting in the spiritual warmth of creative light at New Harmony I could finally see how I was living out the church's violent maledictus. Cursed in the name of Jesus Christ I froze in darkness. In darkness, I became what they named me. "Unhealthy."

When I decided to become a member of my rapist church after attending as an affiliate for six years, I wasn't conscious of my status as a secondary victim in the spiritual rapes committed against Kimberly and Angela. Like all people who align themselves with the primary victim in a spiritual rape, I suffered fallout trauma from both the violence of the church and the trauma reactions of my friends. My response as a secondary victim was, clearly, denial of the obvious truth.

Becoming an official member went against the radical, Jesus Freak fabric of my soul. That's how I framed my reluctance to join. I simply thought of myself as a lone wolf, a maverick, who had to learn to openly align herself with the body of Jesus Christ through church membership. My parents had always joined the Post Chapel or a church wherever we were in the military world. At that time both my parents were Elders in the Presbyterian church where they lived. So, I said to myself, grow up. I went through membership classes, gave my testimony, signed on the dotted line and thereby performed a rite of passage into responsible adulthood. Thus I believed in naive denial.

That's the first church I officially joined in my adult life. Big mistake. Not becoming a member, but choosing that church. Choice is the right word. These are the facts I knew about that church leadership, weighed in my decision and chose to disregard in my denial.

I knew the church leadership consisted of men who had followed the pastor when he split from a mainline denomination over the issue of ordination of women.

I knew the church did not allow women to hold any positions of leadership.

I knew the church had an un-written policy that women could not teach out of the Bible except to other women and children.

The main excuse I used to over-look these ominous facts in my decision to join is that less rigid members of our very large congregation convinced me we needed the "healthy" balance of my "radical feminist" views. Besides feeding my need for denial, this logic appealed to my lone wolf arrogance. After all, the church had tolerated my teaching on the fringe for six years. And I didn't consider myself a radical feminist. As a basic brown bag arrogant, conservative, sexually repressed, Christian feminist I taught about mutual submission, described Jesus as founder of the Women's movement, reframed Paul as a reluctant convert from patriarchal machismo to a believer in sexual equality and went around telling people, "You can't be gay and a Christian". On the fringe, this is healthy.

In the church, I didn't fit anywhere. Imagine that. Two years after I joined I still didn't fit anywhere. Actually, according to the church, the problem was I didn't try to fit anywhere. I remained single, obviously getting older and set in my ways of radical feminist womanhood. I could not possibly have cared less about the "Young Singles Group". They even started a "Career Singles Group" which I successfully avoided. I've never liked being categorized with a herd mentality. Superseding that aversion, I couldn't reconcile my knowledge of Jesus Christ with this church version of a singles bar.

So, I worked for the newspaper, went to school, wrote my plays and failed to fit any of the church molds for acceptable female participation. The first play I wrote was about my relationship with Peggy. It was chosen for the American College Theater Festival. Church people came to see it. A year later they spiritually raped me. I've always wondered about the correlation between those two events.

Ironically, I agreed to be a sponsor for the high school youth group out of this perceived need for me to fit somewhere. Youth sponsor didn't fit either, but it came closer than the singles group for about nine months. Those nine months boil down to this: the kids liked me and my radical feminist teaching, the parents didn't.

The church pastor asked me to meet him in his office one morning in early spring. He announced that the elders had decided I was having unhealthy relationships with the girls in the youth group and wanted me to leave their fellow-ship. I remember feeling confused and asking,

"Unhealthy relationships with whom?"

"With the girls in the youth group."

"The girls, not the boys."

"Yes."

"Are you saying I'm gay?"

"You have unhealthy relation-ships."

"What does that mean?"

No response

In other words, they'd decided I was gay. Me, the valiant sword bearer of conservative Christian all knowingness that says, "You can't be gay and a Christian."

There I was, a fortress of proud conservative Christian celibacy, being given this incredible maledictus by my church. I went into a shock reaction on top of denial. Kimberly took me out and we got drunk on Margaritas. The "unhealthy" twins out on a binge. That was the last healthy relational thing I did until I returned to New Harmony and heard the Goddess whom I later met in the wilderness.

RIDING WILD HORSES HOME

"Every woman stands in the image of Mary when, despite any violence of body or soul done to her, she holds to the belief in her power of love. Through her, not only life but the Christ is born into the world."

Christin Lore Weber
WomanChrist

RIDING WILD HORSES HOME

REMEMBERING THE FALL

I'm heading East into a rose colored dawn, the promise of sunrise in my eyes. Agatha barks at a rabbit scurrying across the road. The healthy rabbit reminds me of a different early morning drive I made one day. In the distance I could see something on the road, so I slowed down. It was a rabbit huddled into itself, with eyes half closed and quivering as if in pain and afraid. A cowboy stood by the side of the road. He smiled at me as I drove carefully around the rabbit in the opposite lane. I thought to myself, "Good. He can see what's wrong and help that poor thing." I glanced in my rearview mirror just in time to see this man kick that helpless, hurting rabbit in a high arc off the road. I felt sick. I pulled over and cried.

The impact of spiritual rape overwhelms like a tidal wave crushing heart, soul, mind and strength. That's where the metaphor ends because when the wave passes there's no wake. There's nothing. Nothing underneath to hold shattered remains. There's nothing except the fall.

In childhood I had a recurring dream about falling. A terrifying dream of falling off a sheer cliff. I could see the cliff face as I fell, faster and faster when suddenly, I landed softly in my mother's favorite chair.

It was a wingback chair upholstered in red and in the dream it stood firmly attached to the face of that cliff. I curled up safely on its seat and knew as long I stayed there, I'd be safe. Then I'd wake up.

When the church spiritually raped me, they threw me out of the chair. That's the only illustration I know for how spiritual rape feels. The violence pierced to the core of my psyche, destroyed all bounds of safe trust and dropped me into a free fall through bottomless fear. After the initial shock, when the Margaritas Kimberly fed me wore off, all I could feel 24-hours-a-day was the dropping and my only perspective was the face of that sheer cliff rushing by. I birthed Aloof to hold me up. He did that by freezing everything in an illusion of control. That left me in frozen darkness, but at least I didn't have to see the cliff face rushing by.

The place in Israel I'd most like to visit is the Garden of Gethsemani because that's where I see the impact of spiritual rape hitting Jesus. He felt the drop and saw the cliff face rushing by, but he never froze. He fell alone through the night in "terrible distress and misery", "My heart is nearly breaking," he told Peter, James, and John. (Matthew 26:37, Phillips) But he never froze. He faced dark violence and won. I'd visit Golgotha because I love the cross and I'd visit the tomb because I hope in resurrection, but if I had to choose one place, I'd choose Gethsemani because I can identify most personally with what Jesus accomplished for us there by allowing himself just to fall.

I, in contrast, wanted to be frozen. I wanted to be numb. I wanted reality to go away and it did along with my creative life. I stopped writing plays. I stopped writing poetry. I wrote papers for school. I reported the news. I journaled. Condemned by community I abandoned community. Creativity abandoned me. I remained a lone wolf, prowling the frozen darkness like a wounded beast.

The church shunned me. People I had known and worshipped with for years simply erased me. I ceased to exist. In my Controlled Impact

Reaction to rape I continued to attend church there believing that I could fix everything by perseverance, by setting a better example for them of how to behave and, by god, I hadn't done anything wrong. I wasn't going to run off with my tail tucked between my legs as if I had. Sunday after Sunday after Sunday I returned. Falling, falling, falling, and aloof in a frozen darkness for which I had no name.

Fortunately, my closest, most intimate friends were people outside the church. Unfortunately, by the time my spiritual rape happened, they all lived far away. Except for Kimberly, none of them knew what was happening to me and even she had no idea of the fall, of the frozen darkness behind my Controlled Impact Reaction. I didn't even tell my mother who is the foundation strength of my life. My father never knew. I watched spiritual rape hurt and change my relationships with everyone around me where I lived. I didn't want that happening to friends far away too. I felt frantic about protecting the people I loved from that pervasive rape ugliness. It was as if a nuclear bomb exploded on me and radioactive waste contaminated everybody connected to my life. So, to preserve my illusion of control, I cut everybody off.

Aloof accomplished this isolation efficiently. I was in love with a man who lived an hour north of me.

Aloof pushed him away. I told him what the pastor had said to me and he wanted to go deal with it but I wouldn't let him. I didn't want it stirred up. I needed control, control, control. Besides, being disfellowshipped did not fit my theology. I wasn't comprehending what this shunning meant. In the end, I knew. I'm real sorry I didn't get the message sooner, before the church had to grab me by the throat, lift me to eye level and say, "Read our collective lips. You're unhealthy and unacceptable. Go away."

When I finally did go away, nobody in the church noticed.

My father died. The youth group girls who had remained supportive of me put an announcement of his death in the church bulletin. My department at the university and the newspaper I worked for both sent flowers and words of sympathy to me out of town at my parent's home. My church, where I'd been a member for eight years, did nothing.

When that unfeeling, power-oriented institution and the people in it ignored not only my grief but failed to honor my father's courageous death after a long battle with cancer, something in me snapped. I knew about death then. I'd gone with my father into death as far as I could go, sitting by his bed waiting for the end for six days, twelve hours a day after his kidneys failed. When I walked into his room at the hospital he said, "I'm dying."

And I replied, "I know Dad, that's why I'm here." So we waited together through the days. My brother sat with him through the nights.

By the fourth day he either slept or wandered through some world apart from me, muttering words connected to memory or emotion. I didn't know where he'd gone. When I knew he wasn't sleeping, I read the Bible to him. He'd requested that earlier, but I didn't know whether or not he could still hear me. I felt my father leaving, like I was watching him walk slowly down a long, long road going away. I felt the separation and frustration of having no control over what was happening to him, to us. Cancer takes control away slowly and insidiously. On the sixth day of our vigil, the last day of his life, in my frustration I asked him, "Dad, do you even know who's talking to you?" He opened his eyes, looked directly into mine and said, "Kitty Unthank." Then he floated away again.

When my helpless father somehow turned around on that long road into death to look at me and speak my name I understood the power of love over death. I remembered Ric. "There are bigger waves down the road." The Goddess held us close during that vigil, through the long good-bye. I remembered who I am in Love's kingdom and when I returned to a church community that had raped and then ignored me I recognized the stench of cancer. Love could not live there. I understood then their desire for me to leave. They had pronounced me unhealthy. By that time, I had become unhealthy. Those people had been right all along. I simply did not belong there. I packed up my aloof heart full of grief and I left.

Death is a bottom line in life, always. Even in frozen darkness falling unconsciously through the wound of spiritual rape, death jerked me up and snapped my head around to see truth, if only for a moment. Soon after my father's death I sought professional help.

Remembering the fall on my way to Peggy I realize the significance of her bottom line, the security it offers as I choose love over hate and go to keep my promise to her. Driving through frozen farmland, pressing through fear to remember the fall, I discover God's gift of faith still present in me, waiting patiently on the other side of that fear. Faith that a bottom line will be there for me when I arrive and look into her eyes.

RIDING WILD HORSES HOME

"In the uncharted forest night, where the terrible wind of God blows directly on the questing, undefended soul, tangled ways may lead to madness. They may also lead, however, as one of the greatest poets of the middle ages tells, to all those things that go to make heaven and earth."

Joseph Campbell
The Masks Of God

RIDING WILD HORSES HOME

REMEMBERING THE CURSE

Remembering hurts. Opening the wound up and dragging bad memories out into the light stinks the place up, like wild horse shit left unattended in the dark would stink. Seems wiser just to leave the wound alone, I think. But I remember all my clients over the years, telling them that in order to recover from their rape wounds they must recover their stories and tell them to me and to each other. Sharing their individual experiences, I explain, reclaims the wound from darkness and brings it into the light to be named. Now, it's my turn alone with Agatha and the wild horses on my way to Peggy who has asked, "What happened?"

The summer Peggy appeared around the corner of the house, before the church spiritually raped me, all my life was an open book. In my arrogant, all knowingness I had nothing to hide from anyone and took great pride in this fact. Peggy and I argued about this openness. She said, "I can't walk down the street holding the hand of the person I love most in the world because the world condemns me for that." I responded, proudly, "I can walk down the street holding anybody's hand I want to because my conscience is clear before God. Who cares what the world thinks?"

"Who cares what the world thinks?" What a battle cry from my innocent young gunslinger mouth. Proud dictus. I believed every word I spoke. The startling truth is that while in the very act of trespassing against God and Peggy with, "You can't be gay and a Christian," my conscience was, indeed, clear before God. I believed I was obeying God by obeying the rules of conservative Christianity, but I was only obeying a god wrapped up in the rules of conservative Christianity, not the God of unconditional love in Jesus Christ. My conscience was clear before a god for all the wrong reasons.

While falling frozen through spiritual rape darkness long hidden things rose to life inside me and were not frozen but had power in simply being remembered. I hadn't forgotten my Uncle sexually assaulting me in childhood any more than I'd forgotten my sexuality. I'd just put them both out of mind and, in arrogant, all-knowingness, out of mind is out of consciousness. Conservative Christianity provides a perfect container for repressed sexuality. Professing belief in the God of Jesus Christ, I instead followed a god who met my need not to have to deal with the sexual part of my being. My wounded sexuality fit nicely into the proud celibacy I rationalized as my service to God. I really believed that my spiritual gifts came to me in direct correlation to how successfully I remained celibate. That's a cozy little empowerment setup for a child victim of sexual abuse. When spiritual rape shattered that illusion of power into dust, when the Goddess began shoveling shit around the roots of my soul in frozen darkness, I didn't know what to do with this wounded sexuality now laid bare before my eyes.

"Maybe the church is right," I thought to myself. "Maybe I am gay." And when that option presented itself to me in the form of comfort in my frozen darkness, I eventually allowed it to happen. I stopped being celibate out of rage at a conservative Christian god who failed to be God, at a church which had already condemned and punished me for this action, and because I had no power to "be good" anymore. Rape always produces powerlessness and powerlessness always produces rage. The only energy left in me after spiritual rape was rage. So, in response to church violence, I became violent. Allowing myself to become sexually active was my way of flipping off god and the church. I thought, for a long time, that this sexually active rage was the worst violence I'd ever committed in my whole life. Then I remembered Peggy.

Remembering feels like being baptized into my own pain; going under this time by choice into the death of the wound. Will I ever emerge free from the power of this darkness? Will I ever emerge at all? "Will you drink this cup?" "Will you remember me?"

I went into three weeks of solitude at The Poet House in New Harmony. I had two immediate needs. Safety and clarity. So, I went the way of the contemplative and entered prayer at New Harmony. I felt safe at New Harmony. Jane Owen generously offered me the Poet

House, as she has to many poet souls over the years, most notably Paul Tillich for whom she has created a special garden memorial. I believe the light and warmth of those gentle souls linger in that place, communing with Jane and whomever she invites to enter. I entered, alone for three weeks, unaware at the time that in those three weeks I stepped across the threshold from frozen darkness into this wilderness where I met the Goddess.

Every morning I sat at the kitchen table to journal and read. One morning I read Psalm 81.

"I hear a voice I had not known: 'In distress you called, and I rescued you. I answered you in the secret place of thunder.'"

I wrote a poem. The first poem I'd written since my spiritual rape.

> Come, hear wisdom
> from within his wounded side.
> Down here deep,
> where the thunder hides.
> Where we contain our rage,
> God and I, together,
> mourning the rape of his Bride;
> whose soul is your soul,
> and whose soul is mine.

The Goddess called to me in this poem, although I didn't know her at the time. I just felt that brief moment of creative surge and felt compelled to write about spiritual rape. But it's her voice.

I can hear her clearly in these words now, having met her in the wilderness. She beckoned to me with this poem, from someplace far, far away as if in the frozen darkness I caught a glimpse of light falling on an ancient, but familiar path home. I've clung to this vision ever since. The path led me thousands of miles away from New Harmony and is long; leading me back, now, to Peggy and the bottom line.

"Will you drink this cup, will you remember me?"

I'm out of M&Ms. Agatha is asleep on the package shelf. It's a hard remembrance.

I needed safety and clarity because the person I finally

sought for professional help in my spiritual rape darkness, the first person I entrusted with knowing how unhealthy I'd become in Chronic Trauma Syndrome was a Christian counselor who seduced me into a sexual relationship. She did this and then, after nearly a year, asked me never to see her again because she'd prayed about it and decided I was, "a mistake."

She's an ordained minister, a professional therapist working in a group of professionals in private practice. She even had a Christian radio show. She knew my wound, she knew I loved her, she knew she had me in a trauma bond and that I would keep her sexual secret. She was right. I did. Faithfully.

When she called to join voice with the maledictus of my rapist church and curse me "a mistake", whatever sense of self I had managed to reclaim in darkness after my spiritual rape was annihilated.

"She must be right," I kept telling myself. "She must be right," I'd say out loud when the pain got so bad I started dying in an agitated depression that had me working 70 hours a week and riding my bicycle endless miles into exhaustion. She was right and I obeyed her. I never called again.

That period of time was the absolute darkest. In the name of Jesus Christ, Conservative

Christianity had cursed me as "an unhealthy gay mistake". By then, I was no longer innocent of the accusation.

Fortunately, I had Aloof in place to keep up appearances and he carried me efficiently along that hellish year. I was sixty pounds overweight, anxiety ridden and confused the night I heard Cris Williamson sing *The Sisters Of Mercy*. Her song marked the beginning of my release from spiritual rape trauma, the year I entered three weeks of solitude at New Harmony and crossed the threshold into this wilderness.

RIDING WILD HORSES HOME

"We know that before a miracle happens there is sorrow, distress, trouble. This reminds us of our weakness, and the mischief that our falling into sin causes. So, we humble ourselves, and fear God, crying for his help and grace. Miracles follow . . . And this is the reason why God is pleased to be known and honored by miracles. He means that we should not be too cast down because of the sorrow and storms that beset us: it is always like this before miracles."

Julian of Norwich
Revelations of Divine Love

RIDING WILD HORSES HOME

REMEMBERING A GIFT

I'm out of the wilderness now,
driving through farmland, appre-
ciating the contrast between
domesticated countryside and the
land I've left behind. No wild
horses here. I'm sure of that. The
two places have only bitter cold in
common. My nose is still running,
my body has begun to ache, I'm
feeling like death and resenting the
physical sacrifice God apparently
deems a necessary piece of this
promise keeping trip.

Jesus started whispering,
"Will you drink this cup? Will
you remember me?" in my ear

about the same time Colorado voters passed Amendment Two. It was a great coup for the conservative Christian power mongers who have set up headquarters in Colorado Springs. I watched TV news coverage of the conservative Christian response, people raising their hands to heaven and thanking God for this victory in the name of Jesus Christ. I expected to feel rage. Instead I felt deep sadness and wept.

Soon afterwards I traveled to Wyoming to lead a women's spiritual retreat. As I stood to begin our encounter a picture tucked back in the corner of the room caught my eye. An artist had drawn Jesus with his face buried in his hands. I recognized him from the feeling I'd felt watching people calling themselves his followers celebrate the violence of Amendment Two.

All eyes followed mine to the picture. I explained my reaction. The older women of that church were touched. They told the story of a loving young woman who had entered their fellowship briefly many years before and brought healing into their lives while she died of cancer. They'd commissioned that picture of Jesus with his face buried in his hands as a way to honor her memory.

"It used to hang right out in the middle of the room so's to be the first thing you'd see coming in here," one old gal told us. "Then they paid to have the place remodeled and without asking us somebody decided to put it back there in the corner."

"You sound angry about that."

"Well, I am. I think all of us who remember her are a little mad."

Nodded assent from around the room. A low rumble that echoes in my soul like pounding hooves on dry earth. I don't ask why they've held this anger in silence so many years. I know why.

"So," I say, "lets move it back to the middle of the room."

And we did. I saw tears in old women's eyes looking at a picture of Jesus with his face buried in his hands. We talked all weekend about what causes Jesus to bury his face in his hands.

Before his death and resurrection the last words heard from Jesus came while he hung on the cross. Among those last words were, "It is finished." Interesting words. I don't know the precise Hebrew, but I'm glad it translates out "finished" and not "over", "done with" or "kaput". Finished means something has been accomplished, refined to its purest form. When God says, "It is finished", you can pretty well bet it is perfect. Whatever "it" is. I wonder about that "it". God knows what God's doing, so, the word choice must be deliberately cryptic. Perhaps the last mini-parable in three dying words. What is finished on that cross BEFORE the resurrection? Jesus could have said,

"It is finished" at the ascension or to any of the 500 people who reportedly saw him after he rose from death. He could have said to Mary, the first to see him resurrected, "Go and tell the others I am risen and that it is finished." That would make sense. But Jesus said, "It is finished", at death. Mysterious last words from a God choosing, at that historical moment, to die.

Jesus chose to die by spiritual rape. Clearly. The motives of Caiaphas and company fit the clinical definition of a power rape to the letter. The high priests had a lot of legitimate god-like power. After all, they manipulated Rome into carrying out the crucifixion of God when both Herod and Pilate were understandably reluctant. That's godlike power. Jesus, being God with a big "G" in the flesh posed a genuine threat to these acting like gods with a little "g" all-knowing priests. So, they killed him. Problem solving with violence. That's the way of the world. It works. And God let it happen.

"It."

Could the "it" of Jesus's last words on the cross be violence? Violence is finished? What is violence perfected, in its purest form? Violence, which is a misuse of power, is a destructive form of energy. Violence perfected by God would be power transformed into creative energy. Jesus allowed the violence of spiritual rape to enter his soul and did not respond with rage. Jesus responded with unconditional love and forgiveness. Before he died, before he rose from death, before he ascended to heaven to sit at God's right hand, vulnerable human Jesus responded to rape with unconditional love and forgiveness. That's a psychological miracle. The final miracle of his life before death and resurrection. The miracle before the miracle we celebrate at Easter. His first miracle turned water into wine at a wedding. His last miracle turned rage into unconditional love and forgiveness at a spiritual rape. No rage. "It is finished." Wow.

What causes this Jesus to bury his face in his hands? How do we trespass against a God who chose death by violence to transform rage into unconditional love and forgiveness? Somebody once asked him, "Which is the greatest commandment?" I could kiss the man who asked this, in my opinion, greatest question ever asked. Every possible thing in all creation balances on the fulcrum of God's answer to this question. Theologically, morally, ethically, spiritually, mentally, physically, psychologically, cosmically, religiously, scientifically, theoretically, philosophically . . . . whatever God says here grounds it all.

"You shall love the Lord, your God, with all your heart, and with all your soul, and with all your mind. This is the greatest and first commandment. And a second is like it: You shall love your neighbor as yourself."(Matthew 22:36-39) At the last supper after washing the disciple's feet, he added, "Love one another just as I have loved you." (John 13:34)

A straightforward answer, I think, as commandments go. Not a suggestion, or helpful hint to apply in situation specific times when humankind deems it appropriate. God said, "Just Do It." Just love God, yourself and others the way Jesus loves you. How does Jesus love us? Unconditionally. Jesus died from spiritual rape loving us, his rapists, unconditionally. That's the rule by which all shall be measured. The law of Christ is unconditional love. How do some people calling themselves Christians manage to so royally screw up this simple commandment?

I know how I managed it. Arrogant knowing. We trespass against God by going around putting conditions on God's unconditional love in the name of Jesus Christ. What else can Jesus do but bury his face in his hands?

On the way home from that Wyoming retreat I stopped in Boulder to attend a Cris Williamson concert. She had come, I think, to sing encouragement to those feeling devastated by the violence of Amendment Two. Between songs she said something to this effect:

"As difficult as this time may seem at the moment, remember

that we are, as a minority, new-comers to this kind of oppression. And we are in good company. As a Native American, the oldest oppressed minority in this country, I encourage you to develop a sense of humor in response to Amendment Two. Native Americans have great sense of humor about their oppression. They've learned it's the way to survive. After all, we are not the enemy they make us out to be and it's up to us to set a better example for them."

I closed my eyes and could see Jesus lifting his face from his hands to smile at her and her words.

The Conservative Christian Coalition, headquartered in Colorado Springs, says, "You can't be gay and a Christian" and turns this arrogant knowing into a political agenda in the name of Jesus Christ. I watched a TV news special about the Conservative Christian movement in Colorado Springs. The camera caught people calling themselves Christians picketing the funeral of an AIDS victim with signs full of violent words reading, "Fags go to hell." "God hates queers." "God sent AIDS to punish perverts."

God sent AIDS. I feel genuine pity for people who will have to stand before God someday accountable for doing such violence in God's name. If God sent AIDS for any reason it's to give those of us calling ourselves Christian an opportunity to respond with the unconditional love and compassion of the God we say we serve. I doubt God has anything at all to do with causing the suffering of AIDS, but if so then all the more reason to hear the Goddess calling us to enter that suffering with comforting words and acts of kindness.

Way up in the corner of Northwest Colorado it comforts me to think that for all the violence Jesus suffers at the hands of the CCC he has the music of Cris Williamson to soothe his divine soul. I believe he dances with her soul as she creates her music and sings to a violent world.

I've been listening to the music of Cris Williamson in the car on my way to keep my promise to Peggy. Actually, I've been listening to the music of Cris

Williamson since Peggy introduced me to her *Changer And The Changed* album that summer she came around the corner of the house. When I was still an arrogant, sexually repressed, conservative Christian know it all on the threshold of spiritual rape, I began listening to the Goddess soul of God coming through this woman's voice. Peggy's gift to me. *The Changer And The Changed.* Peggy knew what my arrogant head could not. I wore that album out in the fall after Peggy left, in those months before the church turned on me.

Through all the years of violence, confusion, rage, dysfunctional relationships, hives, cortisone, sleeplessness and isolation in the agitated depression that followed my spiritual rape, no one single thing did more to sustain me than the music and voice of Cris Williamson. In the middle of it all, while falling paralyzed in frozen darkness, I met her.

She performed at the National Women's Music Festival and I arranged to interview her for the paper. At that time I'd never seen her in person and only knew what she looked like from pictures on album covers. When she entered the room I don't know what my face did while I said, "You're it? You're Cris Williamson?," but she looked immediately offended and replied, "Yes, I'm it. What were you expecting?"

I laughed and told her I'd been listening to her music for so long I was just surprised that such a huge voice came out of such a tiny little person. Then she smiled and told me when she was born her father, standing outside the delivery room, had heard her cry for the first time and said the same thing. "Just listen to that giant voice."

We talked for two hours. Our time together was what Irene Claremont de Castillejo describes as "a real meeting".

"For there to be a meeting, it seems as though a third, a something else, is always present. You may call it Love or the Holy Spirit. Jungians would say that it is the presence of the Self. If this 'other' is present, there cannot have failed to be a meeting. Duration has nothing to do with it. Nor have common interests. The touch of a hand may suffice. I can recall some conversations with total strangers which have never lost their flavor because in some inexplicable way there had for a little while been a real meeting."*Knowing Woman.*

I did not interview her. Rather, we flowed together briefly like the confluence of two rivers, perhaps three because I felt the presence of the divine 'other'. In the end, her entourage came looking for her. I saw them approaching and said, "Here's your entourage." She frowned. "I don't have an entourage." Then turned around and looked up at the group of women standing there waiting. "Maybe I do."

She hugged me good-bye saying, "I want to continue this

conversation another time." Instead of answering "O.K., that would be good," I, in my spiritual rape Aloofness, replied, "No, we'll never see each other again. You know that." She looked perplexed and we parted.

Another quality relational moment in my life, deflecting Cris Williamson's offer of friendship by telling her I know what she knows. There aren't enough M&M's in the world to Band-Aid that moment of arrogance. Jesus not only dropped his head in his hands, I can still hear him groaning.

Since we met I've seen Cris in concert several times. Just before God dragged my wounded soul into the wilderness of Northwest Colorado to meet the Goddess, I attended her anniversary concert and heard her sing *The Sisters Of Mercy* acappella. A captivating performance. Aloof, stunned by consciousness, couldn't deflect the divine message, Rage listened and the wild horses wept.

"Oh, the Sisters of Mercy, they are not departed or gone.
They were waiting for me when I thought that I just can't go on.
And they brought me their comfort and later they brought me their song.
Oh, I hope you run into them, you, who've been travelling so long.
Yes, you who must leave everything that you cannot control.
It begins with your family and later comes round to your soul.
Well, I've been where you're hanging, I

think I can see how you're pinned.
When you're not feeling Holy, your
loneliness says that you've sinned.
I lay down beside them, I made my
confession to them.
They touched both my eyes and I
touched the dew on their hem.
If your life is a leaf that the seasons
tear off and condemn, they will bind
you with love that is graceful and
green as a stem.
When I left they were sleeping, I hope
you run into them soon.
Don't turn on the lights, you can
read their address by the moon.
And it won't make me jealous if I learn
that they've sweetened your night.
We weren't lovers like that and
besides it would still be all right."

Leonard Cohen

173

"Salvation comes to us in the form of a weary traveler."

Henri J.M. Nouwen
With Burning Hearts

RIDING WILD HORSES HOME

REMEMBERING LOVE

I can't say exactly when I stopped falling and the frozen darkness became still. It happened some-time while my isolated hideout in the wilderness slowly evolved into a sanctuary. I walked her wild hills and breathed her high, thin air feeling safe in my solitude. No one could get to me there except God and she enters silently, more gently than snowfall or the full moonlight by which the snow sometimes comes to blanket frozen Earth. In that stillness I heard her voice calling me to remember, to leave my wilderness sanctuary and go keep my promise to Peggy which I'm choosing to do but it's hard.

Two days into the New Year I'm driving a frozen road that takes me, at last, to Peggy's door. There, I discover it's as if she were the sun I've been approaching and when I arrive, I've completely thawed. No more frozen darkness. Just me feeling small and very ill standing on her doorstep.

Peggy opens the door and lets me in out of the cold. She hugs me, stands back and says, "You've gotten so gray!" I think, "Yes, spiritual rape will do that to you every time." But I don't say it. I'm looking into her blue eyes again, remembering.

"You can't be gay and a Christian." And I think, if God can forgive my trespass against this woman's beautiful soul, God can forgive anyone anything.

In the wilderness I live at the Episcopal Church. It's a mission church which can no longer afford to support a full time priest, so, I rent the vicarage from them. I attended this church when I first moved out here because the Episcopal writers I'd been reading made me curious about the denomination. Tentatively, I attended and slowly learned to love the Episcopal service because no matter what other rhetoric may be involved, all worship focuses on the body and blood of Jesus Christ.

Jesus' touching request that we remember him in this specific way centers every Episcopal ritual. They call this celebrating Eucharist. I grew up calling it Communion. In the frozen darkness I felt drawn to his remembrance in this ancient ritual of bread and wine. After spiritual rape, Communion was and still is the only part of being in any church that feels safe to me. I can't attend church where I live anymore because the people who fellowship there voted against allowing openly gay and lesbian people to worship among them. I explained to them that I'd already trespassed against God by telling Peggy, "You can't be gay and a Christian." I will not choose to be part of that kind of violence again. That level of arrogance is too scary for me now, having been there and fallen through years of frozen darkness because of it. I think after the Goddess shoveled all the shit of spiritual rape around my roots I'd be in serious spiritual trouble if I failed to get her message.

I don't miss church but I miss Communion, the conscious action of symbolically joining my soul to the non-violence of Jesus Christ on the cross every time I eat and drink the bread and wine. The miracle is the Goddess bringing Communion to me in solitude, the remembrance of Peggy and my promise to her and hearing His words, "Will you drink this cup, will you remember me?," alive in my soul facing personal violence. I told Peggy she wasn't welcome at God's altar of unconditional love and forgiveness. I said that to her, she believed me and now here I stand looking into her eyes needing to apologize and ask her forgiveness.

I have exactly no energy to carry out this agenda. I left it all on the highway between my wilderness sanctuary and her front door. My long familiar power source of rage is gone and I feel, literally, drained and physically weak.

Peggy has no idea why I'm there nor of the pain that led me to remembrance and this promise keeping. She and her partner just start immediately supplying me with Kleenex and fluids. Agatha rushes into the warmth and tries to connect with their foster dog, Vanna, who remains aloof. Peggy explains that Vanna's elderly owners have fallen ill and she's been recently separated from them as well as the other five dogs in their home. They can't get her to warm up to them.

"Well," I say, looking at Vanna, "she's lost her pack. She's depressed."

Instantly, Vanna gets up, walks over and puts her head in my lap. Aloof, wounded souls recognize one another.

Peggy's partner says, "I can't believe that."

"Believe it," Peggy tells her.

"That's just Kitty being Kitty."

Sick and exhausted, I take a hot bath and fall asleep.

The next morning Peggy and I walk together around an indoor track and she asks what it is I've come to say.

"You remember I told you you can't be gay and a Christian."

She remembers.

"I also promised if God ever showed me I was wrong about that I'd tell you. I'm here to keep my promise. I was wrong about that."

I glance over at her. She just keeps walking with a little smile playing around her mouth. She glances back. "That's it?"

"And I'm sorry. I'm sorrier than you'll ever know that I ever said such a violent thing to you."

Peggy receives my apology with a soft smile and an almost whispered, "Thank-you."

Later that night, over dinner, she says, "You know, I thought you were coming here to tell me you're gay." I laughed and replied, "Who knows? I'm open. But after age 40 it's difficult to start responsibly exploring options. I've been so wounded and repressed in my sexuality for so long, my biggest concern now is not allowing any more violence around that area of my life."

Peggy, in her familiar, exasperated tone of voice demands, "Kitty, do you think you could speak in a way the rest of the world understands and just get to the bottom line?"

So I tell them my story and, I discover, it's easy to tell because all the graves have been marked; my wild horses have their names now and can run free.

At the end I explain, "My coming here to keep this promise to you has nothing to do with me deciding the moral issue of homosexuality. I'm here because I committed an act of violence against God and against the sacred ground of your soul, Peggy, when I said, "You can't be gay and a Christian." I don't know whether you can or can't be gay and a Christian. That's between God and you. All I know is I serve a God of love who chose non-violence in response to human violence and that I face the same choice daily."

Suddenly, I found myself sitting on the bottom line of unconditional love in Jesus Christ saying, with joy rising in laughter through my body at the marvelous simplicity of it, "I don't know and I don't have to know. All I have to know is that I'm commanded to love the way God loves and I think that's what all our lifetime is for, just to learn the basic skills of love."

Peggy sits back and says, "I like this conversation."

Since I arrived at Peggy's to stand on this bottom line of unconditional love I've repeated it to many people and, almost without fail, I hear the question, "So who defines love?"

A lovely moment in which to

remember 1 Corinthians 13.

Love is patient.
Love is kind.
Love is not envious.
Love is not boastful.
Love is not arrogant.
Love is not rude.
Love does not insist on its
own way.
Love is not irritable.
Love is not resentful.
Love does not rejoice in
wrongdoing.
Love rejoices in the truth.
Love bears all things.
Love believes all things.
Love hopes all things.
Love endures all things.
Love never fails.

"Will you drink this cup? Will you remember me?"

RIDING WILD HORSES HOME

"*Real punishment comes to me when I weep tears of grief because I have let someone down. The punishment is not inflicted by anyone else. My own recognition and remorse for what I have done is the worst punishment I could possibly have.*"

Madeline L'Engle
A Stone For A Pillow

RIDING WILD HORSES HOME

UNREMEMBERED

In deep winter when snow covers the ground reflecting full moonlight the night can be as bright as a gray December day. The clarity of such a night reveals a different world; a softer, blended place and in that peculiar, reflecting light I remember those I can't remember.

In the frozen darkness after spiritual rape I hurt these people. I have owned my violence against them and apologized, but the wounds are too great. We remain unremembered except in the forever grace of God in which I hope. As I walk alone in moonlit wilderness nights the Goddess comes to me with memory of my trespasses and we eat and drink that pain in a communion of grief.

If those of us carrying the banner of Jesus Christ, the highest standard of non-violence known to the world, are committing acts of violence such as I have committed in the name of Jesus Christ, what hope is left for the world? While enraged people are killing each other and themselves and our children and us the church points a finger and says, "Well, it's because of those queers out there; those single-parent families out there; those public schools out there; that government out there."

I don't think so. All spiritual people, all churches and denominations, each of us need to look to ourselves. At whom do you point collective fingers of condemnation? What type of person would be too terrified to walk through your door? Who have you pushed away from the communion table of unconditional love and forgiveness in Jesus Christ and kept from remembering him as he asked to be remembered? We're out here. I am just one lone voice in the wilderness, remembering.

"The church needs to recognize that there is another constituency that is also watching. It is made up of those who believe themselves to be rejected by the church. They are the victims of prejudice, those who have been told in word and deed that they do not measure up, do not count, or do not belong. When the assumptions by which this group feels judged are challenged by someone from within the church, they also write . . . They wonder if God or the church has room for them."

John Shelby Spong
Living In Sin?

195

ACKNOWLEDGEMENTS

Thomas Merton, from NEW SEEDS OF CON-
TEMPLATION. Copyright ©1961 by the Abbey
of Gethsemani, Inc.. Reprinted by permission of
New Directions Publishing Corp.

Henri J.M. Nouwen, from THE WOUNDED
HEALER. Copyright ©1979 by Image Books.
Reprinted by permission of Doubleday.

NRSV Bible. Copyright ©1989 by the Division
of Christian Education of the National Council
of the Churches of Christ in the USA. Used by
permission.

Excerpt from **LOVE AND LIVING** by Thomas
Merton. Copyright ©1979 by The Merton
Legacy Trust. Reprinted by permission of Farrar,
Straus & Giroux, Inc.

Marion Woodman, from THE RAVAGED
BRIDEGROOM. Copyright ©1990 by Inner
City Books. Reprinted by permission.

A Table In The Wilderness Daily Meditations
BY: Watchman Nee. Copyright ©1965 by Angus
I. Kinnear. First used by Gospel Literature
Service, India. American Edition published in
1978 by Tyndale House Publishers Inc. Used by
permission of Kingsway Publications, Ltd.,
Sussex, England. All Rights Reserved.

ABOUT THE AUTHOR

Whether teaching colleagues in a professional setting or leading a spiritual retreat, Katherine Unthank always shares this observation: "No matter where we start or what the presenting problems may be, somewhere along the deeply personal paths I'm invited to share with people, the bottom falls out and we're dealing with wounded God space."

As a writer, speaker, teacher and counselor, Katherine Unthank devotes herself to helping survivors of all forms of violence name their personal darkness and find a way home. She earned her undergraduate and graduate degrees from Indiana University in Bloomington, Indiana, is a Licensed Professional Counselor and a National Certified Counselor currently in private practice. She works with both children and adults specializing in Chronic Trauma Reactions. She is also in demand as a speaker and spiritual retreat leader.

In 1998, she and her dog, Agatha, moved away from the Colorado wilderness described in this story in order to continue her spiritual journey toward healing and wholeness. Agatha continues her daily pursuit of comfort. You may communicate with them through Moondrawn Books online: mndrawn@wcic.org

To order *RIDING WILD HORSES HOME: A Conservative Christian Apology,* contact your local bookstore or order directly from Moondrawn Books.

On-Line orders: MNDRAWN@WCIC.ORG

TOLL FREE orders: 1-877-663-7296
                                                MNDRAWN

Fax orders: 1-765-449-0552

Postal orders: Moondrawn Books, P.O. Box 922, Lafayette, IN 47902-0922

Shipping:
$4.00 for the first book and $2.00 for each additional book

Payment:
Check, Credit Card–Visa, MasterCard